SPECIAL DAYS

ISBN 0-7416-1205-4

Published by Havoc Publishing
San Diego, California

Made in China

www.havocpub.com

Havoc Publishing
9808 Waples Street
San Diego, California 92121
U.S.A.

This book belongs to:

_____

...Special notes for January

_____

_____

_____

_____

_____

_____

_____

_____

_____

_____

_____

_____

_____

Celebrate the wonders of this new year. . .

1 _____

_____

_____

2 _____

_____

_____

3 _____

_____

_____

4 _____

_____

_____

5 _____

_____

_____

New beginnings brighten our lives....

6 _____
_____
_____

7 _____
_____
_____

8 _____
_____
_____

9 _____
_____
_____

10 _____
_____
_____

11 _____

_____

_____

12 _____

_____

_____

13 _____

_____

_____

14 _____

_____

_____

15 _____

_____

_____

16 _____

_____

_____

17 _____

_____

_____

18 _____

_____

_____

19 _____

_____

_____

20 _____

_____

_____

21 _____

_____

_____

22 _____

_____

_____

23 _____

_____

_____

24 _____

_____

_____

25 _____

_____

_____

Love and laughter are gifts worth giving...

26 _____
_____
_____

27 _____
_____
_____

28 _____
_____
_____

29 _____
_____
_____

30/31 _____
_____
_____

...Special notes for February

In matters of the heart, let love be your guide...

Love is life's greatest gift...

1 _____
  _____
  _____

2 _____
  _____
  _____

3 _____
  _____
  _____

4 _____
  _____
  _____

5 _____
  _____
  _____

6 _____

_____

_____

7 _____

_____

_____

8 _____

_____

_____

9 _____

_____

_____

10 _____

_____

_____

Make every day a day filled with love...

11 _____

_____

_____

12 _____

_____

_____

13 _____

_____

_____

14 _____

_____

_____

15 _____

_____

_____

16 _____
_____
_____

17 _____
_____
_____

18 _____
_____
_____

19 _____
_____
_____

20 _____
_____
_____

Love someone today in a special way...

21 _____
_____
_____

22 _____
_____
_____

23 _____
_____
_____

24 _____
_____
_____

25 _____
_____
_____

26 _____

_____

_____

27 _____

_____

_____

28/29 _____

_____

_____

March

...Special notes for March

_____

_____

_____

_____

_____

_____

_____

_____

_____

_____

_____

_____

Enjoy your life with friends and family...

1 _____

_____

_____

2 _____

_____

_____

3 _____

_____

_____

4 _____

_____

_____

5 _____

_____

_____

Nurture your seeds of friendship with love...

6 _____

_____

_____

7 _____

_____

_____

8 _____

_____

_____

9 _____

_____

_____

10 _____

_____

_____

11 _____

_____

_____

12 _____

_____

_____

13 _____

_____

_____

14 _____

_____

_____

15 _____

_____

_____

16 _____
_____
_____

17 _____
_____
_____

18 _____
_____
_____

19 _____
_____
_____

20 _____
_____
_____

Be your own best friend...

21 _____
_____
_____

22 _____
_____
_____

23 _____
_____
_____

24 _____
_____
_____

25 _____
_____
_____

26 _____

_____

_____

27 _____

_____

_____

28 _____

_____

_____

29 _____

_____

_____

30/31 _____

_____

_____

April

...Special notes for April

_____

_____

_____

_____

_____

_____

_____

_____

_____

_____

_____

Simple pleasures nurture the spirit...

1 _____
_____
_____

2 _____
_____
_____

3 _____
_____
_____

4 _____
_____
_____

5 _____
_____
_____

Pamper yourself and enjoy every minute...

6 _____

_____

_____

7 _____

_____

_____

8 _____

_____

_____

9 _____

_____

_____

10 _____

_____

_____

11 _____

_____

_____

12 _____

_____

_____

13 _____

_____

_____

14 _____

_____

_____

15 _____

_____

_____

16 _____

_____

_____

17 _____

_____

_____

18 _____

_____

_____

19 _____

_____

_____

20 _____

_____

_____

21 _____

_____

_____

22 _____

_____

_____

23 _____

_____

_____

24 _____

_____

_____

25 _____

_____

_____

Laugh until your cheeks hurt...

26 _____

_____

_____

27 _____

_____

_____

28 _____

_____

_____

29 _____

_____

_____

30 _____

_____

_____

Special notes for May...

Lending a helping hand is rewarding...

1 _____

_____

_____

2 _____

_____

_____

3 _____

_____

_____

4 _____

_____

_____

5 _____

_____

_____

6 _____

_____

_____

7 _____

_____

_____

8 _____

_____

_____

9 _____

_____

_____

10 _____

_____

_____

Do the things that you enjoy most...

11 _____

_____

_____

12 _____

_____

_____

13 _____

_____

_____

14 _____

_____

_____

15 _____

_____

_____

16 _____

_____

_____

17 _____

_____

_____

18 _____

_____

_____

19 _____

_____

_____

20 _____

_____

_____

21 _____

_____

_____

22 _____

_____

_____

23 _____

_____

_____

24 _____

_____

_____

25 _____

_____

_____

26 _____

_____

_____

27 _____

_____

_____

28 _____

_____

_____

29 _____

_____

_____

30/31 _____

_____

_____

June

...Special notes for June

_____

_____

_____

_____

_____

_____

_____

_____

_____

_____

_____

_____

Give the gift of friendship...

1 _____

_____

_____

2 _____

_____

_____

3 _____

_____

_____

4 _____

_____

_____

5 _____

_____

_____

6 _____
_____
_____

7 _____
_____
_____

8 _____
_____

9 _____
_____
_____

10 _____
_____
_____

Enjoy a bouquet of wildflowers...

11 _____
_____
_____

12 _____
_____
_____

13 _____
_____

14 _____
_____
_____

15 _____
_____
_____

16 _____
_____
_____

17 _____
_____
_____

18 _____
_____
_____

19 _____
_____
_____

20 _____
_____
_____

21 _____

_____

_____

22 _____

_____

_____

23 _____

_____

_____

24 _____

_____

_____

25 _____

_____

_____

26 _____

_____

_____

27 _____

_____

_____

28 _____

_____

_____

29 _____

_____

_____

30 _____

_____

_____

...Special notes for July

Take pleasure in little things...

1 _____

_____

_____

2 _____

_____

_____

3 _____

_____

_____

4 _____

_____

_____

5 _____

_____

_____

Tell your friends what you admire most about them . . .

6 _____

_____

_____

7 _____

_____

_____

8 _____

_____

_____

9 _____

_____

_____

10 _____

_____

_____

11 _____

_____

_____

12 _____

_____

_____

13 _____

_____

_____

14 _____

_____

_____

15 _____

_____

_____

16 _____
_____
_____

17 _____
_____
_____

18 _____
_____
_____

19 _____
_____
_____

20 _____
_____
_____

21

22

23

24

25

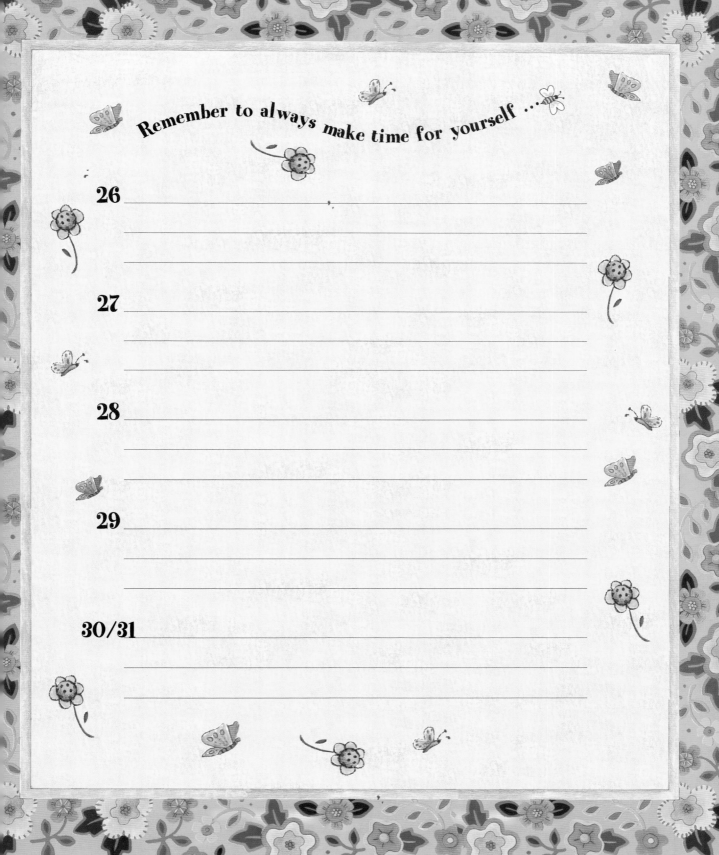

Remember to always make time for yourself ...

26 _____

_____

_____

27 _____

_____

_____

28 _____

_____

_____

29 _____

_____

_____

30/31 _____

_____

_____

August

Special notes for August...

Enjoy a sunset and the star-filled nights...

1 _____

_____

_____

2 _____

_____

_____

3 _____

_____

_____

4 _____

_____

_____

5 _____

_____

_____

6 _____

_____

_____

7 _____

_____

_____

8 _____

_____

_____

9 _____

_____

_____

10 _____

_____

_____

Run through the sprinklers soon...

11
_____
_____
_____

12
_____
_____
_____

13
_____
_____
_____

14
_____
_____
_____

15
_____
_____
_____

16 _____

_____

_____

17 _____

_____

_____

18 _____

_____

_____

19 _____

_____

_____

20 _____

_____

_____

21 _____

_____

_____

22 _____

_____

_____

23 _____

_____

_____

24 _____

_____

_____

25 _____

_____

_____

26 _____

_____

_____

27 _____

_____

_____

28 _____

_____

_____

29 _____

_____

_____

30/31 _____

_____

_____

September

Special notes for September...

_____

_____

_____

_____

_____

_____

_____

_____

_____

_____

_____

_____

Remember the feeling of back to school...

1 _____

_____

_____

2 _____

_____

_____

3 _____

_____

_____

4 _____

_____

_____

5 _____

_____

_____

Be someone who gives really good hugs...

6 _____
_____
_____

7 _____
_____
_____

8 _____
_____
_____

9 _____
_____
_____

10 _____
_____
_____

11 _____

_____

_____

12 _____

_____

_____

13 _____

_____

_____

14 _____

_____

_____

15 _____

_____

_____

16 _____

_____

_____

17 _____

_____

_____

18 _____

_____

_____

19 _____

_____

_____

20 _____

_____

_____

21 _____
_____
_____

22 _____
_____
_____

23 _____
_____
_____

24 _____
_____
_____

25 _____
_____
_____

Remind your family about how special they are...

26 _____
_____
_____

27 _____
_____
_____

28 _____
_____
_____

29 _____
_____
_____

30 _____
_____
_____

October

Special notes for October...

It's time to celebrate color...

Enjoy the sound of walking through leaves...

1

2

3

4

5

6 _____

_____

_____

7 _____

_____

_____

8 _____

_____

_____

9 _____

_____

_____

10 _____

_____

_____

11 _____
_____
_____

12 _____
_____
_____

13 _____
_____

14 _____
_____
_____

15 _____
_____
_____

16

17

18

19

20

21 _____

_____

_____

22 _____

_____

_____

23 _____

_____

_____

24 _____

_____

_____

25 _____

_____

_____

Carve hearts in your pumpkin this year...

26

27

28

29

30/31

Special notes for November...

_____

_____

_____

_____

_____

_____

_____

_____

_____

_____

_____

Gather with family and friends...

1 _____

_____

_____

2 _____

_____

_____

3 _____

_____

_____

4 _____

_____

_____

5 _____

_____

_____

Smile just because you are happy...

6 _____
_____
_____

7 _____
_____
_____

8 _____
_____
_____

9 _____
_____
_____

10 _____
_____
_____

11 _____

_____

_____

12 _____

_____

_____

13 _____

_____

_____

14 _____

_____

_____

15 _____

_____

_____

16 _____

_____

_____

17 _____

_____

_____

18 _____

_____

_____

19 _____

_____

_____

20 _____

_____

_____

21 _____
_____
_____

22 _____
_____
_____

23 _____
_____
_____

24 _____
_____
_____

25 _____
_____
_____

26 _____
_____
_____

27 _____
_____
_____

28 _____
_____
_____

29 _____
_____
_____

30 _____
_____
_____

December

Special notes for December...

_____
_____
_____
_____
_____
_____
_____
_____
_____
_____
_____
_____
_____

Celebrate life with your friends and family...

1 _____
_____
_____

2 _____
_____
_____

3 _____
_____
_____

4 _____
_____
_____

5 _____
_____
_____

6 _____

_____

_____

7 _____

_____

_____

8 _____

_____

_____

9 _____

_____

_____

10 _____

_____

_____

11 _____

_____

_____

12 _____

_____

_____

13 _____

_____

_____

14 _____

_____

_____

15 _____

_____

_____

Keep warm by hugging your friends...

16 _____
_____
_____

17 _____
_____
_____

18 _____
_____
_____

19 _____
_____
_____

20 _____
_____
_____

21 _____

_____

_____

22 _____

_____

_____

23 _____

_____

_____

24 _____

_____

_____

25 _____

_____

_____

26 _____

_____

_____

27 _____

_____

_____

28 _____

_____

_____

29 _____

_____

_____

30/31 _____

_____

_____

SPECIAL DAYS